WILBYE

Oxford Studies of Composers

General Editor : Colin Mason

Egon Wellesz: FUX

Denis Arnold: MARENZIO

Basil Deane: CHERUBINI

Paul Doe: TALLIS

Anthony Payne: SCHOENBERG

Ian Kemp: HINDEMITH

Jerome Roche: PALESTRINA

Norman Kay: SHOSTAKOVICH

Gilbert Reaney: GUILLAUME DE MACHAUT

Roger Nichols: DEBUSSY

Oxford Studies of Composers (11)

WILBYE

DAVID BROWN

London

OXFORD UNIVERSITY PRESS

NEW YORK   TORONTO

1974

Oxford University Press, Ely House, London W.1

GLASGOW NEW YORK TORONTO MELBOURNE WELLINGTON
CAPE TOWN IBADAN NAIROBI DAR ES SALAAM LUSAKA ADDIS ABABA
DELHI BOMBAY CALCUTTA MADRAS KARACHI LAHORE DACCA
KUALA LUMPUR SINGAPORE HONG KONG TOKYO

ISBN 0 19 315220 7

© Oxford University Press 1974

PRINTED IN GREAT BRITAIN
BY W & J MACKAY LIMITED
CHATHAM

PREFACE

JOHN WILBYE is generally acknowledged to be the greatest of the English madrigalists. His output was small—two madrigal volumes containing sixty-four works, and a tiny handful of other compositions— and it is possible, therefore, even in a book of this modest size, to take account of everything he wrote. Nevertheless, because space is restricted, I have resisted the temptation to compare his style and technique with that of his contemporaries except in the most general terms, and the description of his compositional techniques is restricted to those features which seem to me absolutely basic to his style, and without which no study of Wilbye would be complete. A reader who wants a more detailed guide to certain of Wilbye's repetitive procedures may refer to chapter seven of my *Thomas Weelkes* (London, 1969). As for fuller biographical information, the surviving evidence concerning Wilbye was set out very fully by Edmund Fellowes in the preface to his edition of Wilbye's first collection of madrigals (1598), published as *The English Madrigal School*, vol. 6 (London, 1914; revised by Thurston Dart, 1966). This includes a facsimile of the only known document in Wilbye's handwriting.

The original sources of Wilbye's music present it, of course, unbarred, but for convenience' sake when referring to certain passages, I have envisaged it as being written in regular bars of three or four crotchets. In the interests of economy, most musical examples are presented in short score with the text indicated once only in brackets, and a few are in summary form so that certain features may stand out. All have been transcribed from the original sources except for Ex. 10(a), which is taken from the edition of nine madrigals by Ferrabosco, edited by G. E. P. Arkwright, and published in *The Old English Edition*, Vol. 11 (London, 1894).

University of Southampton   DAVID BROWN
April 1973

CONTENTS

To

GABRIELLE and HILARY

INTRODUCTION

ON 7 March 1574 John, third son of Matthew Wilbye, tanner, was baptized in the parish church of Diss in Norfolk. The family was a fairly prosperous one, as their surviving wills make clear, and the area into which John Wilbye was born had long been one of the richest in the country. Nothing is known of John Wilbye's upbringing or of his musical education, but early in his career he entered the service of the Kytson family at Hengrave Hall, a few miles outside Bury St. Edmunds, spending some thirty years of his life there. He also enjoyed contacts with the London musical world, and it was from the Kytsons' town house in Austin Friars that in 1598 he inscribed the dedication of his first set of madrigals.

There had been a strong interest in music at Hengrave long before Wilbye was summoned to the house, and an inventory of 1603 lists a remarkably impressive array of instruments and music books. Wilbye's outstanding gifts obviously found ready recognition from his employers, and he probably also won their respect for his personal character. In her will Lady Kytson made him a substantial bequest of furniture and furnishings, a visible sign of her esteem and gratitude for his long service. By the end of his life Wilbye was a man of considerable means. When he made his own will in 1638 he felt able to style himself 'gentleman' though formerly he had only ranked as 'yeoman'. On Lady Kytson's death in 1628 the establishment at Hengrave broke up. Wilbye, who clearly had no taste for living by himself, now took up residence in the house of Lady Kytson's daughter, Countess Rivers, in Colchester. Here he evidently spent the last ten years of his life. The house is opposite the west end of Holy Trinity Church, where Wilbye was almost certainly buried at some time between September and November 1638. In his will, besides numerous bequests of land, property, and money, there were two musical gifts. To a friend, John Barkar, he left his 'best longe bowe', and most curiously, he bequeathed his 'best vyall' to the future Charles II, then Prince of Wales. Charles was only eight years old in 1638, and so the gift is doubly curious; however, it does suggest that Wilbye may have had some connection with court circles at the end of his life.

There were two main categories of musician in England during Wilbye's lifetime. One comprised church musicians who found employment as singing-men, organists, or choirmasters; the other was made up of domestic musicians who worked as the servants of wealthy families. As a member of the second category, Wilbye was concerned entirely with various kinds of secular music, and his surviving works contain not one example of real church music. A handful of pieces embody religious sentiments, but these were intended for secular, not liturgical use. Wilbye also wrote some consort music, though what has survived is small in quantity and, for the most part, hopelessly incomplete. Considering that he lived a further forty years after the publication of his first collection of madrigals, his output is disappointingly small. We can only surmise that, after the appearance of his second volume in 1609, his interest in composition waned, and when he did furnish two works for Sir William Leighton's *The tears or lamentations of a sorrowful soul* (1614), he provided no more than routine pieces. Thus his reputation rests squarely upon his two volumes of madrigals, and it is with these that the following pages are primarily concerned.

THE MADRIGALS OF 1598

WILBYE and Thomas Weelkes, Wilbye's only peer among the English madrigalists, were close contemporaries. Whether the two men ever met we do not know, though it is possible they may have encountered each other through their known, if irregular, contacts with London. Close acquaintance may be ruled out, for Weelkes passed his whole professional life in the southern counties at Winchester and Chichester, over 100 miles from Hengrave. Yet, even if circumstances had permitted a closer acquaintance, it is doubtful whether the relationship would have been of great musical benefit to either, for just as they were obviously very different as men, so their musical personalities were utterly dissimilar. The world that formed each of them was, of course, the same. Both grew up beneath the shadow of Byrd's towering genius, though since he was over thirty years their senior, the sort of music that he cultivated so magnificently was unlikely to have much use as a foundation for their styles. In any case, while it was the madrigal that occupied both Weelkes and Wilbye at the outset of their careers, Byrd had no great liking for this newly imported style. In his two settings of *This sweet and merry month of May*, included by Thomas Watson in his *Italian madrigals Englished* of 1590, Byrd gave a pointed demonstration that he could encompass a madrigalian manner if he wished, but after that he ignored the form. However, Weelkes and Wilbye could turn for models to the English anthologies of Italian madrigals that had been inaugurated by Nicholas Yonge's *Musica transalpina* in 1588, and which offered a readily accessible fund of continental precedents for their own compositions. Indeed, except for Morley, English madrigalists in general seem to have rarely looked for Italian models outside these London-printed volumes; considering that the madrigal was a thoroughly Italian form, it is perhaps surprising just how completely the student of the English madrigal may ignore the current Italian scene, and treat the English school as an insular phenomenon. In any case, Thomas Morley had been quick to see the commercial possibilities of the madrigal, and from 1593 had produced a swift succession of volumes of his own, thus naturalizing the form into English music, and offering a firm native base upon which other English composers might found their own styles.

For both Weelkes and Wilbye, Morley was the most important formative influence, though from the beginning the restless Weelkes sought a more independent manner, finding in Byrd's contrapuntal example, if not in his actual technique, suggestions for the broadening of his own style. Wilbye's submission to the example of Morley was far more complete, yet he could not remain for long committed to the essential triviality of Morley's canzonet manner, and he probably found the more solemn mien of Alfonso Ferrabosco a useful counterbalance to this. This Italian, who had arrived in England by 1562 and who remained until 1578, composed English-text madrigals which cautiously exposed the essential style of this form without exploiting the more advanced procedures that contemporary Italian composers were already using. Though he was a second-rate composer, Ferrabosco achieved considerable popularity in England, and his pioneer work on behalf of the madrigal was invaluable. Wilbye was certainly impressed by him, and the Italian's influence is most clearly to be seen in the five-voice works of Wilbye's first collection. Joseph Kerman has suggested that it was probably from Ferrabosco that Wilbye took the idea of using reduced scoring in some passages in five- and six-voice madrigals, and also the habit of splitting a composition into two and starting the second half with rather slower music. It is perhaps significant that, although Wilbye set several texts that had already been treated by other composers, the only composer from whom he borrowed not only a text but also some musical ideas was Ferrabosco.

It is impossible to isolate with any precision the other major ingredients that went into the making of Wilbye's style, but it is difficult to believe that George Kirbye did not have a real importance for him. Kirbye published his single volume of madrigals in 1597, the year of Weelkes' first collection, and one year before Wilbye's initial volume; even more important, Kirbye, like Wilbye himself, was a domestic musician living at Rushbrooke Hall, only a few miles the other side of Bury St. Edmunds. It is highly probable that the two men knew each other. Despite his own debt to Morley, Kirbye was a very different creative personality. He was probably older than Wilbye, for a good deal of his music that has survived in manuscript sources is composed in, or is heavily influenced by, the styles of pre-madrigalian English music. It is not surprising, therefore, that when Kirbye turned to the madrigal, he should have cultivated its more serious side. He was an excellent craftsman, and his mastery of the madrigalian technique is thoroughly assured, though the more advanced features of the style find no part in his work. His response to the text, though sensitive, is always very balanced; the symbolic representation of textual details is always precise, but without exaggeration, and the composition flows on freely, yet with easy control. Kirbye had none of Weelkes' imaginative bold-ness, and he lacked the insight that Wilbye was to reveal so impressively in his best works. Among the English madrigalists he was the supreme artisan, absolutely reliable, usually unremarkable, yet capable on occasions of fashioning music that lingers in the memory. His musical personality, with its gentle seriousness and fastidious attention to textural variety, must have found a sympathetic response in Wilbye, and it is difficult to believe that Wilbye's work would have been quite the same, had he not had Kirbye's example before him.

Yet it is unquestionably Morley who dominates the three-voice works which open Wilbye's first volume. Kirbye had printed only four-, five-, and six-voice pieces in his collection, but Wilbye, following the precedent set by Byrd in his *Songs of sundry natures* of 1589 and continued by Weelkes in his first set of madrigals of 1597, included compositions for three voices as well. However, there is a vast difference between Wilbye's three-voice works and their opposite numbers in Weelkes' collection. Since at this stage Weelkes' craft was still very insecure, he plainly decided to channel his most ambitious creative efforts into the three-voice texture, which was the least complicated. In these works Weelkes declines to slip into an unbroken flow of facile, innocuous pleasantries, but shows instead a fierce independence and restless vitality which more than compensate for the passages of poor invention or faltering technique, and which achieves its most striking effect in the pathos of *Cease sorrows now*. Wilbye, on the other hand, never had ambitions either to excite or shock. His models are the three-voice compositions with which Morley had inaugurated his own series of volumes five years earlier, and he works the thematic small change of Morley's canzonet style with complete assurance, generating fluent little sections quite indistinguishable from Morley's own. There is, in fact, little or nothing in any of these six pieces to mark them out as Wilbye's work. Four are structurally as well as stylistically canzonets, employing the normal AABCC form, though one of them, *Weep, O mine eyes* (No. 4) omits the optional middle section (B). *Away, thou shalt not love me* (No. 2) gives a faint hint of the real Wilbye, for it employs a brief extra repetition to unfold an AABBCDD structure, and the stepwise descent characteristic of several of its melodic points does suggest some striving after a more focused expression. Musically, however, the piece is no more ambitious or interesting than the others. Only in one brief passage in *Ay me, can every rumour?* (No. 3) is there a hint of another hallmark of the mature Wilbye, when the upper two voices, having descended in thirds over a held note in the lowest part, then repeat this descent sequentially over another held note (Ex. 1). The sequence is not, however, a strict one, nor is the passage in thirds anything like as distinctive as the best phrases that Wilbye later invented when composing such 'pedal' sequences.

Ex. 1

[Then burst she forth in passion]:

There is, nevertheless, one incidental feature of interest in the opening of *Weep, O mine eyes*. A year later John Bennet issued his only volume of madrigals, borrowing two texts from Wilbye's collection, 'Ye restless thoughts' and 'Weep, O mine eyes'. In neither case did Bennet borrow musically from Wilbye, except at the very opening of *Weep, O mine eyes*. The relationship can be easily seen from Ex. 2. However, Bennet's setting has also an indisputable connection with a second

Ex. 2 (a)
Wilbye (transposed)

[Weep, O mine eyes]

(b)
Bennet

[Weep, O mine eyes]

(c)
Dowland (vocal version, published 1600)

Flow   my____ tears,   fall_____   from your springs

composition, for his treble follows exactly the contour of the opening phrase of John Dowland's most famous composition, *Lacrimae* ('Flow, my tears'), which had already been published in what appears to be its original version as a lute solo in William Barley's *A new book of tablature* of 1596 (Ex. 2c). Only one note need be altered in Wilbye's top voice to make it likewise resemble Dowland's opening. Thus, with the linking evidence provided by Bennet's madrigal, it seems fair to assume that the opening of Wilbye's madrigal is consciously founded upon Dowland's composition.

The three-voice pieces of this first collection are no more than student exercises, but the six four-voice madrigals are real compositions on an altogether different plane. Though each sets a conventional enough love lyric, Wilbye shows himself no longer content to apply the trite imitative formulae from which he had fabricated the three-voice works. Instead he aims at less predictable paragraphs which are far more varied in style and more defined in character, being sometimes quite expansive, but at other times markedly concise.

The readiest way to illustrate Wilbye's inventiveness is to place his *Alas, what hope of speeding?* (No. 9) alongside Kirbye's setting of the same text. Kirbye's piece is sensitive and thoroughly musical, yet it unfolds within a narrow range of procedures so that, though always acceptable, it is by the end a little dull. Neither the music nor the experience ever develops. Kirbye presents the first six lines in five little self-contained phrases, each initially stated by two or three voices and forthwith repeated by the full four voices. A phrase may be expanded on its repetition, but that is about all. As for the last four lines, Kirbye groups them together to make up a final repeated section, with the result that each has an even less substantial character. It is not that Wilbye sets out to produce a weightier work, and he is content to begin with a 4–3 suspension over a tonic-dominant progression, as rudimentary a way of setting 'alas' as you could find. The first four lines are deployed symmetrically enough; none, however, gets quite the same sort of setting as the others, and subsequently Wilbye's paragraphs tend to be more expansive, line 5 being treated at more than twice the length of any of the preceding four lines. As for lines 7 and 8, with which Wilbye begins the second half of his madrigal (following a clean central break after the practice of Ferrabosco), these are overlapped to make a single section that is both extensive and expressively evolving. Despite Kirbye's more pointed musical illustration of certain words, it is Wilbye who reveals the greater variety. By comparison Kirbye seems predictable. In fact, Kirbye's piece is simply an efficient setting of a text; Wilbye's already shows clear signs of a composer who is trying to form a musical experience that transcends the mere matching of words.

Wilbye's technical range is confirmed in *Thus saith my Cloris bright* (No. 11), the text of which is a translation of lines from Guarini. Wilbye sets the first couplet as a large contrapuntal paragraph made from a broadly spaced set of entries which are repeated with the restatement overlapping with the opening in a way that completely masks the fact of repetition. A 'dovetailed' repetition such as this serves simply as a means of expanding a contrapuntal paragraph, but when Wilbye changes abruptly at line three to a series of briefer, virtually homophonic phrases, the reiteration of certain of these serves not merely an expansive function, but is a striking effect in itself. In the four-voice *Lady, when I behold* (No. 10), the use of such 'block' repetitions has become a basic principle of the whole piece. The text of this, too, is a translation from an Italian author, Angelo Grillo, and Wilbye sets it as a kind of expanded canzonet, AABCC becoming AABBCDDEE. No work in this collection has more clearly etched outlines; couple to this the other briefer repetitions and echoes heard within sections (in the central section C these 'internal' repetitions are converted into an extended and very characteristic sequence (Ex. 3)), and the result is a

Ex. 3

[And then behold your lips....]   where sweet love harbours]

piece whose character is very clearly defined. Add to this the clearcut invention, culminating in an especially attractive treatment of the final couplet, and the piece emerges as one of the best and most individual in the whole collection.

Before examining further the separate madrigals of Wilbye's first volume, it will be helpful to turn attention to some more general matters. One of the most fascinating trends in late Renaissance music is the growing concern with structure. The earlier polyphony of the Renaissance had generated works that were characterized by a flow of ever-new invention, but by the end of the sixteenth century composers were manifesting an increasing interest in the creation of rounded musical forms. For instance, many years before Wilbye started composing, Thomas Tallis had shown, in his first set of *Lamentations of Jeremiah*, a quite remarkable insight into the structural function of modulation. The work opens upon E, progressively incorporates B flat instead of B natural, then adds E flat to create an unequivocal B flat major for the setting of 'plorans, ploravit in nocte' before retracing its steps to end, where it began, with a cadence on E. The potency of this extraordinary tritone tension is as great as it is subtle—and the deliberation with which the journey out and back is pursued gives the move not merely an expressive but also a structural function. Wilbye and his contemporaries commanded a technique which freely permitted modulation, yet despite such a precocious example as Tallis' first *Lamentations*, few of them really explored the structural possibilities of key change. One who occasionally did was Byrd—and so, too (though to a lesser extent), did Wilbye. In the three-voice pieces of this collection he made no attempt to do so, being content to restrict himself to casual moves to new keys, slipping mostly into the dominant (and, in minor key pieces, into the relative major), but quickly quitting the new key so that it never had time to develop into a real landmark. However, in each of the four-voice works Wilbye makes at least one modulation that is extended enough to establish firmly a new key in opposition to the tonic. To take the works already discussed: the third quarter of *Alas, what hope of speeding* is set squarely in the sub-dominant,[1] *Thus saith my Cloris bright* has a strong move into the relative major near the middle, and *Lady, when I behold* settles firmly into the relative major towards the end before slipping back into the tonic.

At this period structural modulation was still in its infancy; far more important for formal articulation were the material relationships that a composer might establish between different areas of a work. In Weelkes' compositions there is plenty of evidence of relationships between certain melodic ideas within a single piece, and sometimes he liked to retrace his way freely through an earlier section of a work, producing a recomposition of it to serve as a later section. Wilbye, too, used these procedures. The four-note outline in Ex. 4 underlies several melodic points in

Ex. 4

Thus saith my Cloris bright, and we have already noted that even in such uncharacteristic pieces as the three-voice *Away, thou shalt not love me*, certain simple affinities may be traced between some of the imitative material. Yet thematic relationships play a relatively small part in Wilbye's technique; repetitions and sequences, on the other hand, are absolutely fundamental to it. Such procedures may serve either an organic or a structural purpose. Organic repetition (or sequence) is

[1] In his setting Kirbye remains almost obsessively in one key, with only two very brief suggestions of other keys.

immediate repetition used as a means of expansion and of expressive reinforcement, and became of crucial importance to composers when the decline of Renaissance polyphony deprived them of a technique which fostered a natural growth. The internal, block, and dovetailed repetitions and sequences that we have already observed in the last two madrigals are organic, though block repetitions may also serve structural ends, as in *Lady, when I behold*, where they produce the overall AABBCDDEE scheme. Such short-term repetitions clarify the structure; long-range repetitions, however, integrate it by establishing relationships between widely separated sections. Sometimes Wilbye may freely vary the repetition, as, for instance, at the ends of the two halves of *Alas, what hope of speeding*, where the clear common outline in the treble is supported by quite different harmonic structures (Ex. 5).

Ex. 5(a)

[She at my sighing smiled]

(b)

[Love me, and so deceive me]

In this instance Wilbye has drawn two conclusions together, but in the madrigal pair, *What needeth all this travail?/O fools, can you not see?* (Nos. 7 and 8; the text is an imitation of a sonnet from Desportes' *Les amours de Diane*), it is the central sections of the two madrigals that are related, this time not by variation, but by the incorporation of the same half dozen bars into both (Ex. 6b); the recurrence of the word 'treasure' may have prompted this musical repetition. This explicit formal bond between the two halves is reinforced by other less exact relationships, making this pair of madrigals one of the most integrated of all Wilbye's compositions. The common central passage is itself a product of the work's opening, tracing in retrograde (or inversion) part of this earlier music; in fact, a good deal of the opening and middle areas of both madrigals is based upon derivatives of this basic shape. Ex. 6 sets out these and other relationships. Nevertheless, the closing sections of both madrigals are quite independent, and that of

Ex. 6(a)

[What needeth all this travail and turmoiling?]

[inversion of opening point]

(b) [To seek this far-fetched treasure]

second time

[What ever treasure eye sees]

(c) [Continuation of treble of (b)]

In___ those hot cli-mates, in those hot cli-mates un-der Phoe - bus

(d) [Opening of *O fools*]

O_____ fools, can you not see a traf - fic near — — — — er?

(e) *What needeth?*

Short - 'ning the life's sweet plea - sure

(f)

[To seek this far - fetched treasure]

(g) *O fools*

[O fools, can you not see a traf-fic near - er?]

(h)

In my sweet la - dy's face '

19

O fools is extensive, with an admirable rhythmic life and spaciousness that confirms the very explicit musical character that has been forming itself from the opening notes of *What needeth*, where the firmly shaped lines and strong 'travailing' tread (Ex. 6a) are a whole world removed from the small-talk of the three-voice works. Admittedly Wilbye does use a typical canzonet point to set the second line (Ex. 6e), but he avoids the most obvious brand of contrapuntal treatment, instead repeating it three times in thirds between contrasted pairs of voices, quickly closing each little duet with a tonic cadence, and at the end heading equally firmly to the dominant. Though Wilbye does not confirm this new key at this stage, he cadences in it at the end of *What needeth*, and remains in the dominant region for a long stretch of *O fools*. If the material relationships have bound these two madrigals firmly together, this simple tonal scheme is a powerful agent in establishing a broad structural span over which the pair is firmly stretched.

Between them, *What needeth* and *O fools* compound an impressive experience. But the finest of all these four-voice madrigals is the last, *Adieu, sweet Amaryllis* (No. 12), whose popularity with madrigal singers is fully deserved. Music which can effect such delicate, chameleon-like changes from line to line, yet remain stylistically so assured, can only be written by a composer who is a complete master of his craft. It opens with simple paired subjects which are immediately taken up by the other voices in a way much favoured by Weelkes. But whereas Weelkes would have rotated ostinato-like round these two-bar subjects in pseudo-antiphony to impart a monolithic solidity to the opening (Ex. 7a), Wilbye allows his invention to evolve freely into a variegated section (Ex. 7b) which lingers only to emphasize the pathos of 'adieu' before cadencing firmly in the relative major. To round off the opening paragraph he slips into an *alla breve* manner, concluding with an imperfect cadence back in the tonic. What happens now provides a splendid example of Wilbye's insight. The opening couplet

> Adieu, sweet Amaryllis,
> For since to part your will is,

merely communicates Amaryllis' wish for separation. We may deduce that it is a matter of regret to the poet (and Wilbye's music clearly substantiates this), but it is only in the third line

> O heavy tiding!

that his emotion is made explicit. The imperfect cadence with which Wilbye concludes the opening couplet is, of course, quite unremarkable.

It leads back conventionally to the opening—but it also means that the couplet, after its repetition, remains open-ended, and instead of halting here, Wilbye allows his *alla breve* music to spill over and set the third line, thus swiftly crystallizing, both verbally and musically, the pathos implicit in all that has gone before.

Yet the most beautiful moment is still to come. The opening words return at the end, not only set to a new homophonic phrase, but—far more important—in the major key. This is, of course, a complete reversal of the usual major-to-minor shift used to heighten pathos, but it works perfectly here, giving the closing music a sadness all the more affecting for its aura of resignation. Wilbye was to exploit such minor/major shifts extensively in his second collection. This concluding section of *Adieu, sweet Amaryllis* seems quite different from the opening except that, as Wilbye again emphasizes 'adieu', he slips back into a couple of bars of his opening paragraph before closing with a phrase which confirms that this music *is* related to the opening, for it is a distant paraphrase of the treble of the first six bars (Ex. 7c).

Adieu, sweet Amaryllis is a gem among English madrigals. You will have to look far for another that conveys as much in as few notes. None of the ensuing five-voice works can match it, and the general level of these is markedly lower than that of the four-voice pieces. Several sound like apprentice works, not in the canzonet manner of the three-voice pieces, but in a contrapuntal idiom deriving more from Ferrabosco. Expressively some are almost neutral, ignoring obvious opportunities for characterized expression, and though none is composed in a style that is actually pre-madrigalian, there is much in their expressive restraint that harks back to the sobriety of earlier Elizabethan music.

The opening of the first, *Die, hapless man* (No. 13), illustrates this style very fairly (Ex. 8). The repeat of the opening ten bars suggests the

Ex. 8

structural influence of the canzonet, and the eruption of the alto into a more active line as the repetition begins in bars 11 and 12 of Ex. 8 foreshadows faintly a practice used in some repetitions in Wilbye's second volume. Otherwise the piece has few characteristic features, and it makes excessive use of cadential formulae of the sort heard in bars 7–10 of Ex. 8. In the madrigal pair, *I always beg/Thus love commands* (Nos. 16 and 17), Wilbye employs a two-bar link between the opening section and its repetition, and this link assumes subsequent importance, for it is recalled to launch the second madrigal (Ex. 9a and d). All Wilbye's madrigal pairs in this collection show some concern to relate the two halves and to ensure that there is a musical shape in what might otherwise become very sprawling compositions. This particular madrigal pair reflects the same sort of inter-relationships as *What needeth/O fools*, for material connections may be traced between the first halves of both; in fact, the first twenty bars of *Thus love commands* derive from three separate passages in *I always beg* (Ex. 9). In the case

Ex. 9(a)

[I always beg]

(b)

[I grieve because my griefs are not believed]

(d)

[Thus love commands that I in vain complain me]

(b) *cont.*

(c)

[I always beg]

(d) *cont.*

of bars 3–17 of Ex. 9d it is as though Wilbye had in mind the earlier section of Ex. 9b, and has re-thought it on a far more extensive scale. Such recomposition was used a good deal by Weelkes, too, and we have already noted other examples of similar variations among Wilbye's madrigals. In some instances it seems that the recomposition has been very deliberately designed to produce an explicit structural landmark (as in Ex. 5 above), while in other cases (as in this instance from *Thus love commands*) the earlier passage has merely served as an aural background to the new section, contributing to the consistency of the piece.

I always beg/Thus love commands contains some attractive if not very distinguished music. So, too, does the other five-voice madrigal pair, *I fall, O stay me/And though my love* (Nos. 14 and 15). Again by careful planning Wilbye ensures a clear shape in what is otherwise rather featureless music. In *I fall* he employs a clear textural scheme: full 5vv/upper 3vv, repeated by lower 3vv/full 5vv/upper 3vv, repeated by lower 3vv/full 5vv. *And though my love* is based upon an evolving repetitive scheme:

Line of text: 1 2 3   4 5 6
Musical scheme: A   B–C1–B–D   C2 (extended)

in which the C sections derive from the first three-voice passage in the companion madrigal. Though neither of these madrigal pairs makes much of an impression, some of their counterpoint shows a growing inventiveness and spreads itself more generously, and there is some conventional characterization of the text. A few of the modulations are more assertive than those in the three-voice works, but they lack the purposefulness of the tonal shifts in some of the four-voice madrigals.

Alas, what a wretched life (No. 19) and *Unkind, O stay thy flying* (No. 20) set translations which Thomas Watson had supplied for two Marenzio madrigals printed in *Italian madrigals Englished*. Both are faceless pieces, and technically not strong. The same may also be said of *I sung sometimes* (No. 21); Kerman has observed that the semibreves on 'eye' in this piece may be intended as eye music. *Lady, your words do spite me* (No. 18) is markedly better. The text had already been set by Ferrabosco, and this is the only instance of Wilbye borrowing musically from an earlier setting. His double subject is taken straight from Ferrabosco, though Wilbye pointedly inverts both subjects and works them with far more clarity, preserving their character better than Ferrabosco, who quickly lets them become engulfed in a contrapuntal texture (Ex. 10). After this Wilbye diverges from his model, making the

Ex. 10(a)

Ferrabosco

[Lady, if you so spite me]

(b) Wilbye

[Lady, your words do spite me]

first part of his madrigal almost monothematic by setting the next three lines to points which all derive from the second of his two subjects. Like Ferrabosco, he breaks his madrigal in two. It will be noticed from Ex. 10 that Wilbye's text is not exactly the same as the original; his last four lines are quite different, and he reserves his most striking moment for the very end. Though it seems that the last couplet must have read

So like swans of Leander
Singing and dying my ghost from hence shall wander.

Wilbye transfers 'singing and dying' to the end. It might seem that he has underplayed the almost epigrammatic triple-time setting of these words, but it is perfectly judged, just enough to shroud the departure of the spurned lover's ghost in a fleeting mist of melancholy. Thomas Bateson was evidently impressed with it, and at the mention of 'Meander swans' in *Why do I, dying, live?* from his second collection of 1618, he likewise shifts into triple time. It is difficult to believe that Wilbye did not have in mind Dowland's *Frog galliard*, which had been published only the previous year as the song, *Now, O now I needs must part* (Ex. 11). Wilbye's only known keyboard piece is an arrangement of this very work of Dowland.

Ex. 11(a)

Dowland

Now, oh now I needs must part

(b) Wilbye

Sing - ing and dy - ing, sing - ing and dy - ing.

Yet, good as it is, this madrigal cannot compare with the last five-voice work, *Flora gave me fairest flowers* (No. 22). Instead of the neutral counterpoint from which so many of its companions had been made, this is thoroughly in the style of canzonet, but with lines of purpose and character deployed in concise and distinctive paragraphs to unfold a clear-cut structure. The very characteristic use of repetition and sequence brings this madrigal far closer to the group of four-voice works than to its companion five-voice pieces. *Flora gave me fairest flowers* is a delightful piece culminating in a sparkling invitation to the delights of love which, in its sprightly tonic-dominant alternations, seems to look forward to the age of Purcell.

Wilbye's first collection concludes with eight six-voice pieces whose general level is higher than that of the preceding five-voice works. Admittedly *Sweet love, if thou wilt gain* (No. 23) has no great individuality, but it is a well composed piece whose most notable feature is to be found in the setting of the final line which incorporates two brief passages from earlier in the madrigal, thus effectively drawing together two musical threads. Weelkes, too, recognized the effectiveness of this procedure, and sometimes ended an anthem with an Amen which drew material from the main body of the work. On the other hand, the substantial structural repetition in the madrigal pair, *Of joys and pleasing pains/My throat is sore* (Nos. 26 and 27), was instigated by the text; the final line of *My throat is sore* is

For still the close points to my first beginning

and this prompted Wilbye to set the final couplet to the same music

Ex. 12

that he had used for the first two lines of *Of joys and pleasing pains*, thus neatly framing this very substantial piece. *My throat is sore* incorporates Wilbye's most pungent use of descriptive dissonance, a simultaneous F$\sharp$ and F$\natural$ on 'skriking' to embody the shrill pain of a shriek (Ex. 12).[1] Such an effect is very characteristic of Weelkes and the whole madrigal pair is an impressive exploration of a full-textured vein such as is more readily to be associated with that composer or, even more, with John Ward. In fact, the latter obviously felt this kinship with his own best manner, and when he came to write his own six-voice *Out from the vale*, he had recourse to this madrigal of Wilbye. Perhaps it was the similarity of the eighth line of Wilbye's lyric,

> From hills and dales in my dull ears still singing

to one in his own,

> O'er hills and dales in her dull ears

that reminded him of Wilbye's earlier madrigal pair, and decided him to use, in reverse order, the openings of the two madrigals to father his own settings of the first two lines of *Out from the vale* (Ex. 13).

Wilbye never again attempted a work with quite so much sonorous, dissonance-filled pathos—which is perhaps a pity, for this is a very convincing pair in which even the literal chromatic inflections that invade the music to set 'my song runs all on sharps' contribute to the expressive experience by briefly inflecting the minor with a brighter major. The other work that most nearly approaches this pair in manner is *When shall my wretched life?* (No. 25), though this is consistently *alla breve* with little variety and less inventiveness, the cadential formulae intruding too frequently. Kerman has observed that this is not really a madrigal at all, but is composed in a relatively archaic idiom, perhaps chosen because of the native seriousness of the text. He also points out that the same manner is also used for the six-part settings of similarly serious poems in Wilbye's second collection.

Cruel, behold (No. 28) has pathos at its opening and conclusion. The growth of the madrigal's initial paragraph is particularly impressive, for as the section might be drawing to an end, Wilbye interjects a new, more mobile subject and prolongs the paragraph by working it against the original subject. Subsequently, in the ubiquity of melodic points based upon four stepwise descending notes, the piece shows a thematic singlemindedness which matches that of the first half of *Lady, your*

---

[1] On the other hand, the curious chromatic sixth found a little later (p. 139, bar 5 of Fellowes' edition) seems implausible both musically and as text illustration.

words do spite me. It is a far better piece than either of the works with which Wilbye concludes his volume. *Thou art but young* (No. 29) is a dull piece with a rather silly move to triple time to recall youthful

Ex. 13(a)

Wilbye (1598)

[My throat is sore, my voice is hoarse]

(b)

Ward(1613)

[Out from the vale of deep despair]

(c)

Wilbye

[Of joys and pleasing pains]

(d)

Ward

[With mournful tunes I fill the air]

gaiety on 'O me, that I were young again', and the only features of any interest in *Why dost thou shoot?* (No. 30) are the symmetrical placing of the same three-bar fragment to set 'I yield, sweet love' and 'O hold! what needs?', and the way in which the opening of *What needeth all this travail?* turns up again as the foundation for the setting of part of the concluding line, 'What needs this shooting?'.

The one unqualified success of this group of six-voice madrigals is the remaining one, *Lady, when I behold* (No. 24). This setting is quite distinct from that for four voices, only the last melodic point being shared by both (though, as when he had borrowed material from Ferrabosco for *Lady, your words do spite me*, Wilbye inverts the point). By contrast with the succinct, separated paragraphs of the four-voice setting, those of this six-voice madrigal are fully contrapuntal, with textures as consistently active as any in this collection. This, coupled to the brief use of pseudo-antiphony in the first paragraph, hints at the influence of Weelkes' first madrigal collection; certainly the mastery displayed in this piece suggests that it was one of the last to be written. In the best of the five-voice pieces, *Flora gave me fairest flowers*, Wilbye begins the setting of his last line above a huge descending scale which affords a firm backbone to an active contrapuntal section. A like feature makes the last paragraph of *Lady, when I behold* similarly vertebrate and this, joined to its even richer profusion of imitative incident, makes it the most imposing end to any of the madrigals in the volume.

INTERLUDE

IN 1601 Wilbye was one of the twenty-three composers who contributed to *The Triumphs of Oriana*. Only three years separated this publication from Wilbye's own first collection, but this had been an eventful phase for the English madrigal, above all because it had seen the publication of the remainder of Weelkes' most important contributions to the form. Weelkes' book of five- and six-voice madrigals of 1600 is, with Wilbye's own second volume, the most important in the whole English repertory. We have already noted evidence of Weelkes' influence in Wilbye's first collection, but the impact of these novel, masterly pieces of 1600 upon Wilbye was great, if we may judge from the evidence of *The Lady Oriana*, Wilbye's contribution to *The Triumphs*. This madrigal has an intriguing relationship with both of Wilbye's settings of *Lady, when I behold*, for the opening of *The Lady Oriana* is very like the beginning of

Ex. 14

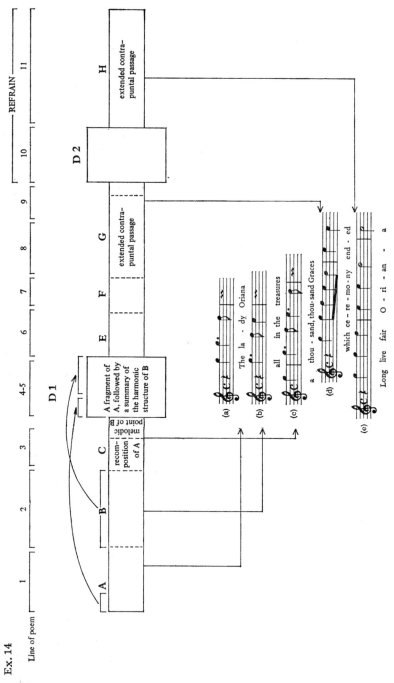

the six-voice *Lady, when I behold*, and the setting of 'Then with an olive wreath' borrows the opening of the four-voice setting of 1598. Could it be that the 'Lady' of the 1598 works was the Queen herself, and that Wilbye was deliberately adapting material from earlier royal works for a new compliment to the sovereign? Or perhaps it was that Wilbye deliberately used material from two of his most characteristic works in order to ensure that his personality was not overwhelmed by that of Weelkes, for he had no wish to become a mere reflection of his great contemporary. What did interest Wilbye were certain of Weelkes' structural practices, and *The Lady Oriana* reflects, more than any other work by Wilbye, Weelkes' ways of structural thinking. Like Weelkes' own Oriana madrigal, *As Vesta was from Latmos hill descending*, the structure of *The Lady Oriana* centres upon two closely related and relatively homophonic sections (D1 and D2 in Ex. 14) which, in *The Lady Oriana*, have some affinity with the opening eighteen or so bars. A diagram is the best way of clarifying the structure (Ex. 14); the simple thematic relationships between the more contrapuntal sections will be noticed. The music of this piece is certainly not the most individual that Wilbye ever wrote, and one wonders whether it was altogether accident that the thematic material to which Weelkes so aptly sets 'came running down amain' should also be used by Wilbye (to set 'which ceremony ended'). When composing this piece Wilbye was obviously aware that it should have a sense of occasion about it, and this may have inclined him towards a resonant contrapuntalism that at times comes close to the magnificent turbulence of Weelkes' best grand manner.

After the appearance of this splendid madrigal eight more years passed before another work of Wilbye appeared in print. When his second collection of madrigals was printed in 1609, the influence of Weelkes upon him had receded. This is not surprising, for even by 1598 many of the essentials of Wilbye's style were already clear, and though he did continue to use some things he had learned from Weelkes, what he did retain he made thoroughly his own. Within the eleven years separating Wilbye's two madrigal volumes Dowland, too, grew to full stature, unfolding in certain of his lute songs expressions of grief and despair unprecedented in English music, and which no later composer ever surpassed. Wilbye must have been impressed, yet as a composer he was even less affected by Dowland, though Kerman has suggested that one of his sequential practices may owe its origin to Dowland (Ex. 15). In his Suffolk retreat he probably found it easy to ignore these new trends, and when his second collection appeared, it

Ex. 15(a)

Dowland: *Come again* (1597)

[To see, to hear, to touch, to kiss, to die]

(b)

Wilbye: *Flourish, ye hillocks* (1609)

[Let me, let me but kiss those steps, those steps]

showed itself to be a natural fulfilment of the first, the expression enriched and broadened, and the insight matured by years of adult experience. Wilbye was now the supreme master of the English madrigal.

THE MADRIGALS OF 1609

WILBYE's second collection of madrigals, like his first, contains groups of works for from three to six voices, thirty-four in all as against thirty in the earlier volume. From the very beginning one is struck by the contrast with the three-voice works of the previous collection. The basic

Ex. 16

[And seeing she is so.....

Lo now I die]

style is still much the same, but the easy chatter of the earlier pieces has been replaced by a far more varied and inventive flow of ideas enriched, where appropriate, by a pathos that is real without being exaggerated. In the first piece in the collection, *Come, shepherd swains*, this is most marked at the end, where two voices moving in thirds above a sustained bass unfold a sorrowful little sequence (Ex. 16). This madrigal sets a four-stanza poem, and since the last stanza opens with the same words as the first, Wilbye is provided with a natural opportunity to return to the opening, thus creating a ternary scheme, though he subsequently passes on to new music so that the expressive experience may evolve to the very end. A similar structural repetition occurs in *Ah, cruel Amaryllis* (No. 3), which sets an English adaptation of some lines by Guarini. Since the verbal recurrence is this time reserved for the very last line, Wilbye dwells at length upon his opening music to fashion a substantial paragraph which is more than a casual nod to the opening. This opening (Ex. 17) manifests a particularly refined chromaticism,

Ex. 17

[Ah, cruel Amaryllis]

the initial B♭ in the alto never recurring until the opening music returns. Tiny chromatic touches of this sort had occasionally occurred in Wilbye's earlier madrigals (such as the B♮ in bar five of the treble of Ex. 7b), but Wilbye's sensitive ear led him to a far greater exploitation of this subtlety in his later works. Sometimes, in a minor key piece, he likes to anticipate the major of the conventional *tierce de picardie* as he does with the C♯s and F♯ in the last four bars of *Come, shepherd swains* (see Ex. 16; Wilbye does exactly the same at the important cadence at the end of verse three, just before the opening music returns). Frequently, however, the major/minor ambivalence is more assertive, as in the centre of *Flourish, ye hillocks* (No. 2), where Wilbye shifts to G minor for eight bars to set 'disdain not love's lamenting', then reverts to the major until, at the very end, a single B♭ brings a fleeting recollection of this earlier incident. This ambivalence is more emphatic still in *O what shall I do?* (No. 6) which, after pursuing its course in G minor, turns unobtrusively to G major towards the end, adds some refined but persistent chromatic colouring on the concluding page, and finally (exactly like *Flourish, ye hillocks*) takes a last momentary glance back to G minor before the final cadence.

This last page of *O what shall I do?* is one of the only two contexts in which Wilbye uses extensive chromaticism, and his treatment of it is very restrained by comparison with Weelkes' extravagant application. Certainly its effect here is far less spectacular than that of the mighty sequence on 'swell' (Ex. 18). Precedents for this can be found in Italian madrigals, but no English composer had ever done anything quite like it. We have already noted how important repetition and sequence are in Wilbye's first collection, but in his second they are even more fundamental, and it is here that the pedal sequence, Wilbye's most characteristic type, emerges fully. This is a form of block sequence for three voices in which the lowest is largely static, often functioning as a pedal above which the other two move mainly in thirds and by step, with a tendency to form suspensions in the latter part of the phrase. The sequence is usually at the second, or at the fourth or fifth. Ex. 19 is an example from the five-voice *Ye that do live in pleasure's plenty*, and the first half-dozen bars of Ex. 16 are also a brief instance of the device.

Ex. 18

will swell

There are so many sequences and repetitions in Wilbye's second collection that it is impracticable as well as unnecessary to remark on every example.[1] As further confirmation of Wilbye's fundamental habit of thinking in terms of these procedures, it is worth observing that he will even use sequence as the foundation of an otherwise evolving

[1] The use of these procedures by Morley, Weelkes, and Wilbye is discussed fully in my *Thomas Weelkes* (London, 1969).

paragraph, so that a multi-voice phrase now fulfils the function of a single melodic point. The opening of the six-voice *Draw on, sweet night*, for instance, begins with a seven-bar phrase for four voices which Wilbye forthwith repeats a fifth lower, and then yet again an octave below the original pitch, all the while ensuring variety by rearranging the voice parts or by adding new counterpoints (Ex. 20a). In fact, if the actual repetitions and sequences of *Draw on, sweet night* are cut, one third of the total work is lost. It is also significant that Wilbye's interest in this second collection has shifted away from repetition (which can merely expand) to sequence which, by moving the reiteration to a new level, can actually make the music progress.

Ex. 19

[Not clogged with earth or wordly cares]

It is the extensive sequences in the central area of *So light is love* (No. 4) that distinguish it from Wilbye's earlier works; otherwise it is not a notable piece. Nor are any of the remaining pieces in this three-voice group as satisfactory as those already discussed, though all have some interest. *As fair as morn* (No. 5) is a curiosity. The bracing freshness of its opening seems far more characteristic of Morley or Weelkes, and it is the only one of all Wilbye's madrigals to incorporate nonsense syllables such as the other two composers had frequently used. Perhaps the real clue to Wilbye's intention is found at the end, with its exaggerated contrasts between sprightly quavers on 'She smiles. Fa la' and sustained semibreves and minims on 'Ah, she frowns', for such extreme juxtapositions, quite untypical of Wilbye, are a marked characteristic of Weelkes. Possibly Wilbye was poking gentle fun at extremes which his poised personality must have found rather ridiculous—though in fairness it must be remembered that Weelkes had himself apparently satirized exaggerated madrigalian grief in his three-voice *Ay me, alas, hey ho*, published the previous year. Nevertheless, the possibility that Wilbye had the work of his great madrigalian peer in mind is increased by the triple-time section which he interjects into

Ex. 20(a) | *Large notes show sequential foundation; small notes indicate free additions.*

(a)

That   do   arise]

(b)

this madrigal. Such sections were common in Weelkes' madrigals, but rare in Wilbye's own.

The last two three-voice works must be taken together, for the second, *There is a jewel* (No. 8), is labelled *rispòsta*, and provides an answer to the questioning of *I live, and yet methinks I do not breathe* (No. 7), a lyric based upon lines from Petrarch. This association is confirmed by a four-bar phrase which the two pieces have in common, though this relationship seems half-hearted when compared to similar instances amongst Wilbye's other madrigal pairs. The lyric, *There is a jewel*, has a positively pre-madrigalian flavour with its unctuous commendation of the virtues of being contented, and this may have induced Wilbye to bias towards a neutral expressive manner in his music (though the 'homely whistle' gets due musical acknowledgement). The result is not one of Wilbye's better works, though it is worth noting the sequence on 'seldom it comes', made from a one-bar cell repeated over a slowly descending bass which functions rather like a cantus firmus (Ex. 21). This 'cantus firmus' form of multiple sequence was used by Wilbye more elaborately in some other madrigals. Nor is *I live, and yet methinks* especially notable, despite its more consistently madrigalian character. Its most striking single moment is the chromatically-based wrench between phrases to reflect the 'uncouth jar' of the text.

The madrigals in Wilbye's second collection must have been

composed over a far longer period than those of the first. Of the pieces in the four-voice section of this second volume it seems probable that among the earliest is *I love, alas* (No. 14) and, possibly, *As matchless beauty* (No. 15). The latter is a charming but straightforward canzonet which, nevertheless, reveals one trait very characteristic of the mature Wilbye when, on the repetition of 'Thou diest in him' (initially sung by three voices), the fourth voice adds a simple but effective counterpoint. Much of *I love, alas* is equally in the style of a canzonet, but it has no initial repeat, and the repetition of the concluding couplet is modified so that, while the last line is musically the same both times, the preceding line receives quite different settings. Like some of Wilbye's earlier works, this one splits into two and opens its second half with rather slower music after the practice of Ferrabosco. The setting of the final line, with its strongly labouring sequence, recalls the opening of *What needeth all this travail* from Wilbye's earlier collection, using a thematic outline which turns up in about one quarter of the works in that volume, but nowhere else in this second set. It would be easy to believe that *When Cloris heard* (No. 9), which shares a brief section with *I love, alas*, is also rather earlier than some of its companions; however, *Happy streams whose trembling fall* (No. 10) could never have belonged to the earlier collection. The pseudo-antiphony of the opening might conceivably have done, but the bold transference of the opening eight bars up a third into the relative major for their repetition resembles nothing in Wilbye's first volume. This opening is one of the most enchanting in all Wilbye's work, and little that follows quite matches it, good though the remainder of the piece is. The madrigal begins and ends in D minor, but the whole central area is firmly seated in the major (first G, then D), the most equal balance of major and minor that we have so far encountered. The purpose of this contrast is not dramatic, however, but colouristic, the brighter major reflecting the blessed relationship of birds and streams to the beloved, and the return to the sadder minor, allied to an *alla breve* conclusion (and a single beautiful chromaticism in the treble), conveying the grief of the rejected lover.

A marked feature of some of these four-voice works is the exploration of a more virile and enterprising contrapuntalism which both enhances the character of a section and aids its organic growth. There are strong signs of it in *Happy streams*, but it is more fully displayed in the opening of *Change me, O heavens* (No. 11), whose text stems from a verse of Luigi Grotto. At the text's instigation the sharply profiled initial point is promptly 'changed' the other way up so that the forceful descending sixth becomes an even more powerful rising sixth, and Wilbye lets fly with a set of unceremonious entries, splendidly maintaining the character of the music, refusing to confine his point within one neat little paragraph, and making the second section grow almost seamlessly out of the preceding one, its supple, firm point generating a paragraph as impressive as the first. As in *Happy streams*, the opening turns out to be the best part; indeed, the decline in quality of *Change me, O heavens* is far sharper. There is a characteristic pedal sequence in the centre of the piece, but this gives way to a resurgence of a more conventional canzonet style. Only at the very end does the employment of a more firmly shaped melodic point restore a little of the opening's character and strength.

The most athletically contrapuntal of all Wilbye's madrigals is *Fly not so swift* (No. 13). The upward rushing scales at the beginning are a conventional enough representation of the text, but the melodic point goes on for a further full bar, amplifying and fortifying its character; the point to 'if not a smiling glance' is equally extensive, Wilbye using its rushing quavers to generate a splendid turbulence (Ex. 22). The manner remains as buoyant as that of the canzonet, and 'see how they coast the downs' almost reverts to the simplest canzonet manner, but the equally light point used for the next line quickly crystallizes into a form some three bars long, distinctive in character, and used by Wilbye to generate an extensive paragraph. The text is splendidly handled. No one can take the lover's 'dying' and 'crying' very seriously, and Wilbye keeps a clear sense of proportion: a deft slide into a brief *alla breve* section, a single light chromaticism, and the lover's lament is perfectly placed in perspective (see Ex. 22).

Yet even such a felicitous treatment must yield to that of *Love not me for comely grace* (No. 12). Of all Wilbye's qualities, none is more remarkable than his ability to match the *whole* experience of a text. This was something quite beyond Weelkes, whose most active response to a text results in, at most, a succession of musical incidents reflecting

single words or phrases. Such a response is at the most obvious level, and Weelkes' strength as a setter of words lay in the capacity of his vivid imagination for turning what was really a stock response to a particular word or phrase into a brilliant musical conception. If the text did not contain such opportunities for direct musical representation, Weelkes normally produced a generalized setting. Wilbye, too, respected the details of his texts, but he also could absorb the whole experience to a degree that none of his contemporaries, except Byrd and possibly Dowland, could equal. Perhaps this is one of the reasons why Wilbye showed so little interest in developing further the devices for musical integration that Weelkes had exploited, and which he himself appeared to be absorbing in his Oriana madrigal. Weelkes was constantly aware of his music as music which should have its own shape; Wilbye was prepared to let the text prompt a developing musical experience which might encompass the whole piece, thus ensuring an expressive evolution that reduced the need for a purely musical logic.

Love not me for comely grace sets a lyric which views woman's perverseness in love with a cynicism that is far removed from any Petrarchan convention. Instead it conveys an accumulating bitterness,

Ex. 23

and it is this dynamic growth of feeling that Wilbye matches so successfully. The guileless homophonic opening might lead the listener to expect the lightest of madrigals, but the expression grows in weight as the work unfolds in the increasingly firm madrigalian counterpoint of

Wilbye's mature style. This positive growth is reinforced by a change to tonic major for the latter part of the piece, and at the final line Wilbye bursts briefly into a stern (but not forbidding) canon at the octave—and also by inverted diminution (Ex. 23, bars 7ff). Thus is conveyed in purely musical terms the seriousness beneath the surface, and by the end a penetrating reflection of the emotional state of the poet has been achieved.

It has long been recognized that late Renaissance English music shows a clear distinction between an Italianate line with its roots in the madrigal, and a persisting native tradition which perpetuates the more sober and serious aesthetic of pre-madrigalian English music. What is not always sufficiently acknowledged is just how much even the most radical exponents of the passionate and dramatic Italianate style still owed to their native background. After all, most, if not all, of the schooling of English composers at this period was in the techniques of indigenous music. Morley, in his Latin settings that have survived in manuscript sources, shows just how thoroughly he for one had mastered the native manner, and even when he transferred his allegiance to the madrigal, the pull of his old habits was strong, and there was a marked resurgence of native elements in some pieces of his last madrigal collection of 1597. Weelkes, too, was drawn towards a contrapuntalism which owed more to English than Italian precedents, and much of his best music is a synthesis of imported and indigenous elements. Even Dowland in his most extreme compositions retained powerful traces of native English song. One need look no further than those three remarkable songs with treble viol obbligato, published in his last collection of 1612, for the viol does nothing to heighten the expressive temperature by imitative collaboration with the voice, but instead follows its independent and undemonstrative path just like many viol parts in early Elizabethan consort songs. Even in Dowland's most intense works many vocal phrases have a step-wise progress and measured breadth which is far closer to the vocal manner of these same consort songs than to Italian monody.

This mixture of Italian and native English manners is often elusive, but it can be clearly sensed in the last of Wilbye's four-voice works, *Happy, O happy he* (No. 16). This is the most self-consciously serious of all, the text dwelling upon a favourite theme of earlier Elizabethan poets—the happiness of the man who eschews worldly things for a life of worthier aspiration. Wilbye's setting is likewise redolent of a pre-madrigalian manner, utterly devoid of any trace of the canzonet idiom, yet remaining, for all its restraint, truly madrigalian. The splendid growth manifest in the setting of the first two lines matches the corresponding section of *Change me, O heavens*, but this time Wilbye manages to maintain the level of the opening, passing through a wonderfully calm setting of 'in silent peace his way to heaven prepares' to end with a stately pedal sequence, on the last statement of which the treble adds a new counterpoint which sinks finally through a 'weary' chromaticism that sets the seal upon this noble piece.

Unlike their counterparts in Wilbye's first collection, the five-voice works of this set do not show a falling-off in quality, for even the least interesting, such as *There where I saw*, *Ye that do live in pleasure's plenty*, and *A silly sylvan* (Nos. 24, 25, and 26), are excellently written pieces. The last of these has the half-way break with ensuing slower movement which suggests the lingering influence of Ferrabosco, and the very extensive setting of the second line appears to draw upon the substantial last paragraph of Weelkes' madrigal, *Now is the bridals*, printed in his collection of 1598. But whereas Weelkes builds a freely evolving contrapuntal web (though filled with tiny internal sequences), Wilbye characteristically constructs much of his vast section around three-voice block sequences with the voice parts redistributed and supplemented to create genuinely evolving music. Wilbye binds the two halves of his piece together by briefly using material from this passage during the latter half of the work. *There where I saw* is quite as carefully wrought, with unstrained alternations of *a note nere* and *alla breve* sections, and the tonal inflections so typical of Wilbye's maturity. It starts firmly in A minor, moves equally positively to the relative major in line two, visits G major in pseudo-antiphony, touches the flat side of the tonic in D minor and then, in a series of sorties into sharper regions, finally reaches A major for the setting of the last line.

Yet, for all its impeccable taste and tonal variety, *There where I saw* lacks that distinctiveness of invention that lodges certain of its companion works so firmly in the memory. Perhaps some portions of *Ye that do live in pleasure's plenty* do linger on; its brilliant extravert manner is certainly effective, but there seems little beneath the surface, and the superficiality is not really countered by the pedal sequence that briefly interrupts the prevailing brightness (see Ex. 19).

The madrigal pair, *Down in a valley/Hard destinies* (Nos. 21 and 22), does possess some of this individuality, though it misses the level attained by the remaining five-voice works. Wilbye does not seem to be much concerned with integrating devices in either of his five-voice madrigal pairs in this collection, certainly not in the way he is in the other paired works we have examined, though it is difficult to believe that he did not deliberately devise a musical frame to *Down in a valley*, for the opening melodic point, which shapes out before our eyes so clearly a descending sequence of little valleys, recurs freely in the last line in augmentation and in ascending form. There is no quotation from earlier material in *Hard destinies*, but its end has the effect of conflating elements from *Down in a valley*, the *alla breve* manner of that madrigal's conclusion being used, but now growing around a melodic point rather closer to the shape of that with which the whole piece had begun. It seems that this end, in its turn, served as a sketch for a portion of *Draw on, sweet night*, for the latter opens with an expanded version of this conclusion a fifth lower (see Ex. 20b). One marked feature of all these last four five-voice madrigals is Wilbye's liking for launching a new phrase with an abrupt change to an E major chord, normally following a cadence in C major. Though by no means exclusive to Wilbye, of course, the frequency with which he used the device makes it a minor fingerprint of his style. Its effectiveness is unfailing, and one cannot avoid a suspicion that Wilbye sometimes deliberately had recourse to it when his inspiration was rather limp or faltering.

There remain five five-voice madrigals, all of which rank with Wilbye's very best compositions. *Weep, weep, mine eyes* (No. 23) reveals the same grasp of the dynamic power of modulation as does *Happy streams*, for Wilbye repeats the opening eight-bar phrase a fourth higher in the subdominant (and then yet again in modified form with a further fourth shift), though the effect this time is not a heightening of delight, as was the minor-to-major move in the four-voice piece, but an intensification of tearful restlessness. Tonally, too, there is differentiation between the two halves of the piece, as well as Wilbye's characteristic major/minor ambivalence. It starts in D major, thus establishing a sharp-key area, modulates to G major with a touch of C major, and returns to D with a slide into the minor at the very end of the first half. D minor is extended into the second half with the relative major now exercising the tonal pull, thus setting this portion of the work in a quite contrasted key area to that of the first part, though there is a resurgence of D major at the centre to make the defiance of death the more positive. The agitated, repeated-note declamation on 'Ah, cruel fortune', with its flanking exclamations, 'Ay me', shows a strong influence of monody, and is one of the most overtly Italianate passages in all Wilbye's work (Ex. 24). Yet its obvious dramatic effectiveness must not be allowed to distract attention from Wilbye's masterly realization of the emotional content of the remainder of the lyric, with its firm defiance of death and its hope of joy in the Elysian hereafter—a blessed state anticipated in happy little sequences which wind down to the final cadence.

Ex. 24

The text of *All pleasure is of this condition* (No. 19) is a verse translation from Boethius. Like *Love not me for comely grace*, this is a madrigal that expresses a constantly evolving experience, starting with pleasure and the lively buzzing of bees, and ending in pain and sorrow, reflected in the most weary, gloom-ridden music that Wilbye ever wrote. He dutifully mirrors 'pleasure' with quavers, 'pricks forward' with a syncopated phrase in which two voices tread on the heels of another voice, thus nudging it forward until its 'fruition' is finally signified by the attainment of the dominant. The bees buzz most audibly, but always very musically, in Wilbye's most impressive cantus firmus sequence, finally departing in two flights of quavers, but leaving a sting expressed in the melodic and harmonic tensions of an extended paragraph; the ubiquitous falling seventh is but one of these. Finally the 'gnawing grief and never-ending smart' is marvellously treated in a three-stage section of which the centre is one of Wilbye's simplest but most impressive pedal sequences, its effect enhanced by the sudden change of register for the first sequential restatement, and its weariness perfectly matching the text.

There is no such obvious expressive evolution in *Oft have I vowed* (No. 20), but Wilbye unobtrusively sets the piece into instant motion, not by establishing the tonic and then moving outward from it, but rather by the reverse process of starting in an unstable tonal situation and then progressively asserting the tonic. Thus the piece begins with only the lightest hint of the tonic G minor before shifting to the relative major and then quickly moving out even further to F major, finally heading back to the tonic at the end of the first couplet. After a conventional representation of 'sighs' at the beginning of line three, the music rejoins quite literally that of line one (though now in the tonic itself) until, at the end, the phrase is extended to 'remove' to the relative major again. In line four the tonic at last achieves its absolute supremacy, and over a massive dominant pedal Wilbye uses an appropriate multiplicity of repetitions of 'millions of tears' to confirm G minor in one gigantic perfect cadence. The setting of 'suff'rest my feeble heart to pine with anguish' is, with the end of the three-voice *O what shall I do ?*, the only piece of extended chromaticism in all Wilbye's work, though there is no hint either of tonal instability or, indeed, of modulation, for the chromaticism of the individual lines is far from total, and the bass ensures that the whole passage resides firmly in G minor (Ex. 25). The final twist to G major to set 'my bitter days do waste, and I do languish', like the end of *Adieu, sweet Amaryllis*, produces a resigned melancholy rather than self-pity, though two brief chromatic slides in the last bars add final twinges of extra pathos, as well as echoing the earlier chromatic passage.

Ex. 25

Yet the most impressive of all these five-voice works is the pair, *Sweet honey-sucking bees/Yet, sweet, take heed* (Nos. 17 and 18), whose text derives from the Dutch writer, Jan Everaerts. The total effect of this piece is the more surprising because it starts with the lightest of canzonet openings, though the way in which Wilbye modifies the initial repetition is enough to show that he has no intention of falling back on easy, stock procedures. The pseudo-antiphony of the opening recalls Weelkes; even more does the long delay in the bass's entry, a feature of several of Weelkes' madrigals. But otherwise the work is quite unlike Weelkes. This is the sort of piece that tempts rhapsodic prose—and which therefore really needs it least of all. Suffice it to comment here upon the vitality and freshness of Wilbye's invention, the rhythmic flexibility, and the constant variety of scoring. To take just one point: note how the alto and tenor cannot restrain their excitement, bursting in with a hectic duet on 'there may you revel' two and a half bars before the end of the previous section, only to be joined in full-throated chorus by all voices before a trio is left to complete the phrase. *Yet, sweet, take heed* is deployed as two large five-voice flanks separated by a huge block repetition based upon a phrase which, through internal sequences, grows to a full thirteen bars. No passage in all Wilbye's work shows better than this the tensile strength and character with which he could inform music of a style which a lesser composer could so easily make trivial (Ex. 26). The occurrence of 'sharp' in the text

Ex. 26

[For if one flam — — — ing dart come from her eye....

Was nev - er dart so sharp, ah,——

—— then you die!——]

provides a natural cue for a final shift to G major for one of Wilbye's most impressive major-key conclusions, a strangely autumnal setting of 'Ah, then you die!', more affecting than all the self-dramatizing hysteria or self-pity of more conventional madrigalian prognostications of death.

Sweet honey-sucking bees/*Yet, sweet, take heed* is a magnificent piece by any standards. It is remarkably buoyant, is often gay and brilliant, and its pathos is of the lightest, yet it has the strength of sprung steel. Of all English madrigals of bright and extravert character, this is perhaps the finest. With two notable exceptions the six-voice works in the collection are less interesting than most of the preceding pieces. The first three set serious, quite unmadrigalian texts for which Wilbye provides music that retains much of the solemnity of pre-madrigalian English music, though often enriched with a lavish use of suspended dissonance that belongs far more to a madrigalian idiom. The opening of *O wretched man* (No. 27) might have been prompted by the beginning of Weelkes' *Methinks I hear* from his six-voice madrigals of 1600, but whereas Weelkes continues with a varied succession of musical images, Wilbye never moves far from the expressive world established by this opening. Neither grief nor pleasure receives special musical emphasis; instead the piece unfolds largely as a succession of stately block sequences and repetitions, finally coming full circle as the opening music returns to set the final line. This is a more interesting piece than the pair of compositions that follows it, *Where most my thoughts/ Despiteful thus unto myself* (Nos. 28 and 29). The setting of the opening couplet is largely built from a string of cadential formulae, and a good deal of what follows is faceless; the most characteristic touch is the progressive penetration into sharp keys during the setting of the final couplet so that a predominantly minor key piece ends in the major. Yet this move, even when coupled to the more mobile music that Wilbye provides for this passage, seems no more than a forlorn effort to vivify a lifeless piece. *Ah, cannot sighs?* (No. 30) is better; its most striking feature is the poignant setting of the last line which exploits a bold type of dissonance which might more readily be associated with Weelkes (Ex. 27). *Long have I made these hills* (No. 34), a better piece still,

Ex. 27

[Was never grief like mine]

also has some overtones of this composer, for its strong double subject generates a broad initial paragraph that has a massiveness reminiscent of Weelkes, and its subsequent course reveals some studied contrasts of the sort in which Weelkes revelled. Similarly *Softly, O softly drop, mine eyes* (No. 33) is a good piece, though lacking that individuality of invention that might win it a place amongst Wilbye's best pieces. The setting is careful but not illuminating. Kerman has observed that the poem is possibly the most exaggerated Italianate love lament in the whole English madrigal repertory, but adds that Wilbye's setting is entirely innocent of parody.

However, the remaining two works must rank with Wilbye's very best pieces. Like *Love not me for comely grace* and *All pleasure is of this condition, Stay, Corydon, thou swain* (No. 32) is a work that evolves expressively, though the trend of *All pleasure* is reversed, for it starts with slowly moving music and ends with the utmost animation. It reflects initially the despair of a lovelorn and rejected Corydon, and concludes, after the dispensing of some sound advice, with a vigorous amorous pursuit of this same Corydon by the formerly disobliging nymph, a close chase enthusiastically represented by aptly sequential imitation in which the participating voices follow on one another's heels at a mere one-beat's distance. The result is one of Wilbye's most irresistible pieces.

Yet this—and, indeed, all Wilbye's other works—must yield place to the remaining madrigal, *Draw on, sweet night* (No. 31), a piece which, oddly enough, starts with music very similar to that which opens *Stay, Corydon, thou swain*. We have already noted the blend of Italian and native English manners in *Happy, O happy he*, but in none of Wilbye's works is it more effective than in *Draw on, sweet night*, for while the piece is a true madrigal, it has a breadth of paragraph and gravity of utterance that have a strong affinity with music of the indigenous tradition. Its emotional intensity may stem from Italian precedents, but its melancholy is completely English. The sequential foundation of the opening paragraph has already been observed (see Ex. 20a), and throughout the piece less veiled sequences deepen the melancholy, or add further weight to the burden of sorrow that seeks its comfort in darkness. Constant variety of scoring contributes to the aura of the music, as do the alternations of tonic major and minor; nowhere does Wilbye exploit this latter device as deliberately or as powerfully as here. *Draw on, sweet night* is another of those pieces that tempts eulogistic prose, but which declares itself so eloquently as to render effusion unnecessary. Nevertheless, the structure of the piece does require some comment. Expressively it grows from two elements. The first of these is the sustained D major music through which night is invoked, the second the more animated D minor music treating the second couplet and reflecting the turmoil of a man whose 'life so ill through want of comfort fares'. The recurrence of the opening words in line five is an obvious cue for a return of the opening music, but the repetition is far from literal; instead Wilbye meditates upon his opening bars, amplifying the experience and devising in the course of this one of the

Ex. 28

loveliest contrapuntal additions to be found anywhere in his work (Ex. 28; for the opening, see Ex. 20a). The succession of three-voice sequences that follow upon this section[1] might suggest that Wilbye is now intending to follow the normal madrigalian practice of moving onwards through new musical material, but this is not to be, for during the setting of the penultimate line there are heard with increasing clarity echoes of the music that had set line two, until Wilbye finally sweeps on to set the last line to a close variant of the music that had earlier set line three (Ex. 29), brooding upon it at length until the final

---

[1] It is difficult to believe that the discrepancy between the top voices in the first sequence is correct, despite the original 1609 print and its perpetuation in the recent revision of Fellowes' edition. It seems most probable that the version in the sequential repetition is the correct one, and that the initial statement should therefore conclude thus (Ex. 30):

Ex. 30

Ex. 29(a)

[That do arise from painful melancholy....

(b) *(outlines only)*

[And while thou all in silence dost enfold....

(a)

(b)

(a)

My life so ill through want of comfort fares,]

(b)

I then shall have best time for my complaining]

cadence. Expressed schematically in the simplest terms,[1] the relationships appear thus:

Line of text:

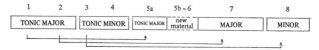

1	2	3	4	5a	5b – 6	7	8
TONIC MAJOR		TONIC MINOR		TONIC MAJOR	new material	MAJOR	MINOR

Draw on, sweet night is another Wilbye madrigal in which the whole setting is a penetrating realization of the very essence of the poem, achieved this time far less by expressive evolution (as in *Love not me for comely grace* or *All pleasure is of this condition*) than by an oscillation between the music of night and the music of the tormented man, a restless interaction which finds no easy resolution in the final cadence. It was not in Wilbye's nature to cry out in unrestrained despair as Dowland could, but here he achieves an expression of deepest human melancholy, purged of all maudlin self-pity, that is quite as profound and serious as anything in Dowland's greatest songs. *Draw on, sweet night* by itself would be enough to establish Wilbye as one of the most distinguished composers of his time. It is not only his masterpiece and the greatest of English madrigals; it is one of the most beautiful pieces ever written by an English composer.

CONCLUSION

There is little to add. Neither of Wilbye's contributions to Leighton's *The Tears or lamentations of a sorrowful soul* (1614) is of much importance. The first, *I am quite tired with my groans*, may also, like *The Lady Oriana*, take its departure from the six-voice *Lady, when I behold*, and there can be little doubt that when Wilbye wrote the opening of his

---

[1] A more elaborate schematic analysis is included in my *Thomas Weelkes* (London, 1969), p. 133.

second Leighton contribution, *O God, the rock*, he had in mind the music to which he had set the second line of *Draw on, sweet night*, but in neither case did he manage to match the quality of these madrigals. A faint hint of the same passage from *Draw on, sweet night* may also be detected in the opening of Wilbye's brief viol-accompanied solo song, *Ne reminiscaris*. This is one of the small group of Wilbye's compositions that survive solely in manuscript sources. None is of great importance, though the quietly expressive setting of *Homo natus de muliere* has some real distinction. *O who shall ease me?* (which unfortunately survives incomplete) is also better than either of the Leighton pieces. The dullest of these manuscript compositions is the six-part fantasia. Certainly it would appear that all the very best music Wilbye ever wrote is to be found in his two madrigal collections.

We have no way of knowing why Wilbye wrote virtually nothing during the last twenty-nine years of his life. Presumably the Kytsons did not press him to compose, but there was no reason why he should not have written more madrigals specifically for the English musical press, even if his employers had lost interest in the form. Fellowes suggested that when Wilbye was granted a lease on a valuable sheep farm in 1613 his interests shifted to the cultivation of material rather than artistic riches. Yet by itself this appears an insufficient reason; it seems far more probable that he simply felt he had nothing to add to what he had already written. Had he lived in London he might have been exposed to stimuli and pressures which could have tempted him to explore new musical territories. But he was a provincial musician, and as he looked at the musical scene around him, he may well have felt that the world was passing him by. His highly sensitive yet poised personality could never have engaged in the mercurial or dramatic brilliance that Weelkes had already so stunningly exploited (and abandoned). Though Wilbye was capable of profound melancholy, there is no murkiness in the half-light of *Draw on, sweet night*, and he could never have followed Dowland into the turbulent shadows or the black night of despair, nor have emulated the sombre sonorities of Ward. Nor could the witty trivialities of Weelkes' *Ayres* of 1608, or the heartier pieces of Bennet, Ravenscroft, and the like, have found any creative response in him. From all we know about Wilbye, it seems that he was a wise man; if, indeed, he felt that he had achieved in his two madrigal volumes the best of which he was capable, then he never showed greater wisdom than in not breaking his silence.

SELECTED BIBLIOGRAPHY

Brown, D., *Thomas Weelkes: a biographical and critical study* (London, 1969).

Collet, R., 'John Wilbye: some aspects of his music', *The Score*, 4 (June 1951), pp. 57ff.

Fellowes, E. H., *The English madrigal composers* (London, 1921; second ed., 1948).

Fellowes, E. H., *English madrigal verse, 1588–1632* (London, 1920; rev. enlarged ed., 1967).

Fellowes, E. H., 'John Wilbye', *Proceedings of the Royal Musical Association*, vol. 41 (1915), pp. 55ff.

Gage, J., *The history and antiquities of Hengrave, in Suffolk* (London, 1822).

Heurich, H., *John Wilbye in seinen Madrigalen: Studien zu einem Bilde seiner Persönlichkeit* (Augsburg, 1931).

Kerman, J., *The Elizabethan madrigal: a comparative study* (New York and London, 1962).

Tovey, D. F., 'Wilbye and Palestrina: four sixteenth-century motets', *Essays in Musical Analysis*, vol. 5 (London, 1937), pp. 12 ff.

LIST OF WORKS

Madrigals:

The first set of English madrigals to 3, 4, 5, and 6 voices (London, 1598).

The Lady Oriana (a madrigal contributed to *The Triumphs of Oriana* (London, 1601)).

The second set of madrigals to 3, 4, 5, and 6 parts, apt both for viols and voices (London, 1609).

(The standard modern edition of these is edited by Edmund Fellowes in *The English Madrigal School*, vols. 6 and 7 (London, 1914 and 1920; revised by Thurston Dart in 1966).

Consort song:

Ne reminiscaris, 5vv (British Museum MSS., Add. 18936–9, 29366–8 and 29372–7. Printed in *Musica Britannica*, vol. 22, edited by Philip Brett (London, 1967)).

Settings of religious texts:

Two contributions to Sir W. Leighton, *The Tears or lamentations of a sorrowful soul* (London, 1614):

1 *I am quite tired with my groans*, 4vv
2 *O God, the rock of my whole strength*, 5vv
(Printed in the complete edition of Leighton's volume, edited by Cecil Hill as *Early English Church Music*, vol. 11 (London, 1970), and also in *The English Madrigal School*, vol. 6).
Homo natus de muliere, 6vv (Bodleian MSS., Mus. f1–6. Printed in *The Old English Edition*, vol. 21, edited by G. E. P. Arkwright (London, 1898)).
O who shall ease me?, 6vv (lacks 2vv; Bodleian MSS., Mus. f20, 22–4).
Instrumental music:
Fantasia, 6vv (Dublin, Marsh's Library MSS., Z 3.4.7–12. Printed in *Musica Britannica*, vol. 9, edited by Thurston Dart and William Coates (London, 1955; revised ed., 1962)).
3 fantasias, 4vv (altus only survives; British Museum MS., Add. 29427).
The Frog galliard [John Dowland]: set for keyboard by Wilbye by August 1612 (Clement Matchett's Virginal Book. Printed in an edition by Thurston Dart (London, 1957)).